HOW TO GET WHAT YOU REALLY WANT

Norman W. Wilson PhD

HOW TO GET WHAT YOU REALLY WANT

Cover Design by

www.srwalkerdesigns.com

A ZADKIEL PUBLISHING PAPERBACK

ISBN: 978-1-78695-150-2

Zadkiel Publishing
An Imprint of Fiction4All
www.fiction4all.com

This Edition
Published 2018

INTERIOR PHOTOGRAPHY

SUZANNE V. WILSON, PHOTOGRAPHY

DEDICATION

This little book is dedicated to all those who have made intentions and failed BUT who continue to make the effort to bring their intention(s) into reality. You can succeed.

OUR INTENTION CREATES OUR REALITY

Dr. Wayne Dyer

CHAPTER ONE
WHAT IS AN INTENTION?

Brenna Yovanoff in *The Replacement* writes "Intention is one of the most powerful forces there is. What you mean when you do a thing will always determine the outcome. The law creates the world." The most powerful force there is? What a pronouncement that is.

An intention is a state of mind in which there is a commitment, a fulfilling of a particular action, or desire. Furthermore, intention involves mental action involving planning. This is simply another way of saying commitment. According to WORD, commitment means binding yourself intellectually and physically to a course of action. The significant word in this definition is *binding*. Three words, commitment, action, and binding must be married if you are to enjoy any hope of fulfilling your desires. One without the other two guarantees disappointment—failure!

Fundamentally, intention is a function and as such, it is one that is designed to accomplish a very specific task or thing. All too often, we make our intention too generalized in stating what it is that we want, desire, or need. When you come to understand the internal functions of intention you will then be able to apply those to your daily life. Zack Michael in "Be Grateful for Every Step (my view)" [August 25, 2017] tells us to not only focus on the end[goal], focus on everything in between with gratitude inside. More will be said about gratitude in Chapter Seven.

Many books, articles, and even a movie provide an incomplete picture. If the montage was complete, people wouldn't continue to seek how to make an intention and to have it bear fruit. Instinctively, I feel there is something lacking—some wondrous secret of secrets. Because I feel this way, this book is really dedicated to the proposition that you can change your destiny, you can bring into reality that which you want.

Intention is the mechanism by which you can bring into reality that which you desire. In a later chapter, I will be discussing the mechanism of intention. Just as an automobile has an engine, wheels, body, gears, a source of energy to function so likewise does intention have its necessary components in order to function.

Dr. Bruce Lipton reminds all of us that "Matter and energy are entangled. Mind and body are similarly bound." [1] All things are energy including the earth, the universe, co-existing galaxies, and we humans. In The Soul's Journey to Its Destiny, Swami Ashokanada says [Man's] "physical being is a part of the universal matter." From my perspective, herein lies the secret of secrets.

Remember, an intention is a goal. Perhaps *vision* better describes what takes place. You see or visualize a future event and it is that which becomes your guide for your activities, that is, what you experience. A gentle reminder at this point is appropriate: your intention does not have to be limited to material things, for instance, money or a new car. Your intention can relate to your health, physical and emotional. It can be for peace, the success of a community project, or the health of a loved one. There is no limit as to what your intention may be.

The question now is why is intention important?

> There is always a gap between intention and action.
>
> Paulo Coelho

CHAPTER TWO
WHY IS INTENTION IMPORTANT?

A road map was designed to provide you choices of routes you could take to get from one point to another. An intention is a road map upon which you have identified your goals, prioritized them, and have indicated which one you want to pursue. Your road map becomes a declaration to the Universe that you mean business. The Universe does not like generalities.

Pre-thinking, clear-thinking, and positive thinking are essential in building your road map. It allows for specificity, that is, it brings identification to who you are as well as what it is you desire. Once you have set a clear ad purposive intention you will discover yourself acting in ways that actually are in harmony with your intention.

Without positive intention the likelihood of your just wandering from one thing to another, one job to another, one relationship to another increase in manifold ways.

Philosopher Elizabeth Anscombe in an essay titled *Intentions* (1957) says intention is central to one's understanding of him or herself. One of my favorite writings from antiquity is the Brihadaranyaka Upanishad. There, in IV4.5 is a wonderful comment that is applicable to intention. It reads "You are what your deep, driving desire is. As your desire is, so is your will. As your will is, so is your deed. As your deed is, so is your destiny." Use the first line as your personal mantra by switching it to the personal pronoun. *I am what my deep, driving desire is.* Beautiful, totally beautiful! Here is another mantra that you may find helpful. I recommend saying the mantras anytime you wish but especially just before going to sleep and the first thing in the morning.

Don Juan, Carlos Castaneda's teacher, said: "*…in the universe there is an immeasurable, indescribable force which sorcerers call intent, and that absolutely everything that exists in the entire cosmos is attached to intent by a connecting link.*" [2] Two things in this statement are significant: First is the notion of an indescribable force called intent and second is that of a connecting link. According to some writers in the field, this indescribable force is universal consciousness, that is, the universe is a living, breathing, entity. The connection to this "indescribable force" called intention is humankind. I think this "immeasurable" force is energy. All things are made of energy, both animate and inanimate. All thought is energy. It takes intention to direct this energy. Simply put, human beings with their intention direct this universal energy. And if this is true, you can easily see how one can bring into reality one's desires by intention. However, there must be a balance, a harmony between you and your internal desires.

The bottom line is intention is what makes the world go around. It's the mechanism that fires up the workings of the Universe.

Live less out of habit and more out of Intent.

CHAPTER THREE
MAKING SURE YOUR INTENTION IS POWERFUL

Aren't all intentions powerful? This is a legitimate question. My answer is an emphatic no! Unfortunately and all too frequently people enter into the world of making intentions half-heartedly. The attitude of the individual making an intention is extremely important. The Universe in its infinite wisdom will not waste its time bringing forth an intention that is not upworthy. This becomes realistic when you take into account the world's population of 7.5 billion people and their demands on the Universe.

Jo-Ann Downey in *How to Create Powerful Indentions* states "To create powerful intentions you need the correct ingredients and ample time." [3] Downey also says "Intentions can be general or very specific and they can be on any level." I disagree with that. As I pointed out in my book, Shamanic Manifesting [4], the Universe does not like generalities.

From my perspective, here's an example of a general intention: "Help me." Help you with what? Emotions or physical issues? With material issues? Creating a weak intention most certainly guarantees failure. Ten years ago, Mario Beauregard and Denyse O'Leary reminded us that "experiments have shown that, because your brain is a quantum system, if you focus on a given idea, you hold its pattern of connecting neurons in place." [5] All you have to do is to release that pattern into the Universe.

American poet, Ralph Waldo Emerson put it this way, "Once you make a decision, the Universe conspires to make it happen."

Deepak Chopra reminds us that "Intention is the starting point of every dream." [6] It is also the mechanism for turning that dream into reality. A sure way to make that wonderful dream fail to materialize is to confuse intention with goal-setting. Declaring your intention is not the same a goal setting. Don't misunderstand. Setting goals are fine but it is different from intention. In goal setting, your efforts are directed at seeing the future, at understanding what you desire. It's a way to stay on track, so to speak. For example, you want to increase your sales during the next six months. Your efforts, skills, and work are all directed to obtaining your goal. To accomplish your goal, you increase your mailers, build your email accounts, have an open house, offer specialty items on sale. Marla Tabuka issues a warning. She states, "For those who set goals and sometimes fail to achieve them, the act of goal setting can lead to a sense of, not only failing but of being a failure."[7]

Intention, however, is very much focused on the *now.* Author Phillip Moffitt says, " You set your intention based on understanding what matters most to you and [you] make a commitment to align your worldly actions with your inner values." [8] Moffitt warns you that cultivating intention does not mean you give up goal-setting. I suppose another way of putting this would be to say goals are what you focus on and intentions are what you do about them. A cautionary note is appropriate at this point. Goals should motivate you—if they don't, you have selected the wrong goals. And as with intention, failure is caused by flawed instruction. Here's an example of a flawed instruction: *Think of yourself living your dream and it will be yours.*

It is all too easy to forget "an intention is represented in the end result you want to achieve—the present tense or what you want today, and your future to look like It is not a 'to-do-list'. [9]

To help you with this, I recommend the use of the Gyan Mudra. This particular hand posture helps to bring an openness that allows receptivity. In traditional Ayurveda, the Gyan Mudra boosts what is called the "air element." This "air element" stimulates and empowers the mind and enhances one's concentration.

Here is an illustration of the Gyan Mudra hand position. Use either hand or both hands.

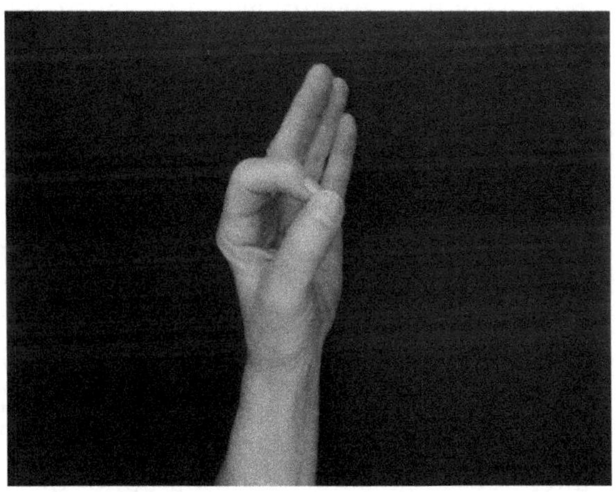

Psychologist and author Dr. Christian Jarrett in "How Goals and Good Intentions Can Hold Us Back" states, new research shows that intrinsic motivation thrives when you focus on your immediate experience rather than the end game. At first glance, this may appear to be contradictory of what has been written about making intentions. It is not! One of the secrets to making intention work is to visualize it as already existing. It's very present oriented and not future based as in *someday down the road attitude.* Dr. Jarrett continues by saying there is "a major downside" if one stays focused on goals. That downside is the experience of the activities you use are spoiled, that is, you are hell-bent on the goal as a consequence all the richness of the experiences to reach that goal is lost.

A gift of intention initiates the process of creation.

One question frequently asked by those about to begin serious intention work is based on the notion of positive vs negative. How can a person have positive intentions and still commit terrible things? Author and behavioral technologist, Robert Dilits states "Having good intentions is not a guarantee of good behavior." [10] Dilts, a highly regarded advocate and promoter of Neuro-Linguisti c Programming, also states "People who have good intentions do bad things because they have limited maps of the world. Problems arise when a well-intended person's map of the world presents only a few choices for satisfying their intentions. A simple work-around this is to make the following concept a basic and integral part of your core beliefs—do no harm—do right.

Do not create an intention with the sole purpose of bringing harm to another. What you intend will come back to you. The Universe is nonjudgmental. It does not make decisions based on human moral percepts good and evil. It does not make a determination if something is good, bad, or indifferent.

Some may view the power of intention with total skepticism and others dismiss it altogether as woo-woo. There is a growing body of scientific based information demonstrating intention works. One of the more recent studies was conducted by Dr. Masaru Emoto. He proved beyond a reasonable doubt that water, for instance, can be influenced by intention. What this means is that our physical world can be influenced by thought.

Arjun Walia states "Consciousness can be a big factor in creating change on the planet. Sending thoughts of love, healing intent, prayer, good intention, and more can have a powerful influence on what you are directing those feelings toward." [11]

Believing in negative thoughts is the single greatest obstruction to success.

CHAPTER FOUR
CONSCIOUSNESS AND INTENTION

"The idea of consciousness has intrigued philosophers from centuries, but it has resisted a simple definition. Philosopher David Chalmers has cataloged more than twenty-thousand papers written on the subject."(Micio Kaku) [12]

Dean Radin, Ph.D., Chief Scientist of the Institute of Noetic Sciences in 2016 introduced the results of a series of experiments that may provide the missing link between consciousness and matter, turning the tables on materialism and asserting consciousness as a fundamental component of reality itself. [13] The implications are tremendous—consciousness creates matter—material substance extracted into reality by conscious intentions.

The purpose here is not to provide either a scientific or psychological treatise on consciousness, but rather to highlight some of the more significant and relevant areas of mutuality. What then, is consciousness? I suppose the immediate definition of consciousness is simply being alive. Merriam-Webster provides the following definition: *the quality or state of being aware especially of something within oneself.* Definitions also include being aware of objects outside of oneself.

"We are made up of a countless number of atoms.[seven billion billion billion or that's followed by 27 zeros.] As a result, we are energy-creations beings by default. It is our belief, along with many others, that energy stems from consciousness. And this consciousness is connected to the material world." [14]

From a psychological view, c**onsciousness** refers to our awareness of our own mental processes, such as our thoughts, feelings, and sensations thus giving one the ability to introspect, or look inward and examine those processes. The diagram below shows a general construct of the brain. Note the average adult human brain weighs in at three pounds. It contains approximately 100 billion neurons. If these were put end to end, they would reach out 600 miles. Your DNA would reach to the moon. I point out these figures just to show how marvelously complicated the human brain is and that its potential is literally unlimited. You have a lot to work with when it comes to making your intentions into reality.

I want to repeat don Juan's statement in Carlos Castaneda's *The Power of Silence: Further Lessons of don Juan,* don Juan says, "In the universe there is an immeasurable, indescribable force which sorcerers call intent, and that absolutely everything that exists in the entire cosmos is attached to intent by a connecting link." [15] For me, that connecting link is consciousness. Without it [consciousness] there is nothing. Arjun Walia points out that many of the founding fathers of quantum physics all shared the same belief: Consciousness is fundamental, that is, it precedes material reality. [16] For those of you who need to know, the founding fathers of quantum physics include Albert Einstein, Max Plank, Neils Bohr, Werner Heisenberg, Erwin Schrodinger, a Wolfgang Pauli just to name a few.

Enoch Tan in a post at *Mind Reality.Com* made the following observation that is worth repeating here. "We think through universal consciousness and since it is universal, all thoughts generated on a personal level are a part of the sum and total of all thought—therefore, what you think into existence receives the attention of all minds—making the reality you want." I strongly suggest you think about this because it is so powerful.

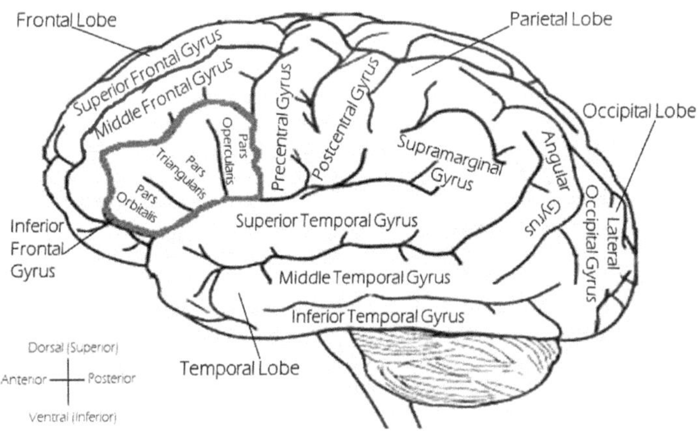

Supposedly, there are three areas of the brain that have a direct connection to consciousness: the brainstem, a spot just under the left temple, and deep behind the center of the forehead. [17] It appears that the brainstem functions as the point of arousal. One can't help but draw a connection to the Third Eye as the same area behind the center of the forehead.

CHAPTER FIVE
INTENTION AND THE THIRD EYE

Those who are knowledgeable about the chakras will recognize the Third Eye as the sixth chakra. Here is an illustration of the human Third Eye Chakra. [18] It is located between the eyebrows, about an inch up the forehead. The Third Eye is frequently referred to as the Mind's Eye or as the Inner Eye. According to John J. Ratey, author of *A User's Guide to the Brain,* the biological foundation of the mind's ey is not fully understood. The fundamentals for the basis for the Third Eye is found in the deeper part of the brain just below the neocortex—where the center of perception exists. It is suggested that the pineal gland produces the Third Eye.

The pineal gland is a cone shaped organ and is located behind and just above the pituitary gland. It is interesting to note that the pineal gland contains pigment similar to that found in our eyes and further, it is connected to the optic thalami. It is believed that the joining of the essential substances of these two glands in the third ventricle is actually what opens the Third Eye.

The Pinal gland functions in two ways: First, it is responsible for activating adolescence and for preventing premature sexuality. Second, the pineal gland inhibits the immediate discharge of thoughts into action. This allows us to look inward and to think and evaluate our actions. This introversion is indispensable for self-realization as it displaces our attention from the outer world to the inner. [19]

Because of this introversion, the Third Eye is fourth dimensional. Being a receiver and transmitter, many different types of vibrations can be translated, integrated, and or delivered to what we call our "normal" world. It is here that your intention is brought into reality. With an open Third Eye, you open your intuition and then have the opportunity to feel the language of your intention.

Besides opening the Third Eye to bring your intention into reality, it opens the potential for telepathy, clairvoyance, lucid dreaming, and astral projection. As with many physical things in today's world of food, air, and water contamination with GMOs, the pineal gland has the problem of calcification because of the introduction of fluoride and calcium phosphate in our diets. Fluoride is used in dentistry and in drinking water. Artificial sweeteners, hormone additives, radiation from electronics in our homes, and of course, our cellphones.

Andye Murphy in his article titled "How to Awaken Your Third Eye [20] (edited by Kendra Sand) suggests an assignment to help get your Third Eye working again.

Actually, Murphy suggests three activities.

Activity One:

Be grateful you have a pineal gland. Send gratitude to your Third Eye for you innate intuitive abilities. Do this every day.

Activity Two:

Spend ten minutes each day during which you consciously activate your Third Eye through meditation, chanting, prayer, dance or yoga.

Activity Three:

Sun gazing is an excellent source of power. Gently gaze at the sun during the first few minutes of the sunrise and the last few minute of the sunset. This is an easy way to boost your pineal gland and to get your Third Eye working.

Jewelie and Casey Kochmer in "What is the Third Eye?" [21] point out, and rightly so, the Third Eye has several possible uses. Among these, they list the following: Sense and visually interpret energy around you, see motion-activity, and exchange of energy, sense and project potential, and of course, intention. Here are some strategies used to open the Third Eye. First, and this is perhaps the most difficult to achieve in today's busy world is silence—mind silence. Second, polish your use of intuition by paying closer attention to your dreams, hunches, gut-instincts. If you are in a parking lot try guessing which way other shoppers are going or how many people will enter a restaurant within a given amount of time, say fifteen minutes. Third, play guessing games and keep track of how many times you have guessed correctly. Try increasing the number of correct guesses. Fourth, mindfulness meditation helps hone your sensitivity. Specifically, visualize the color indigo while you are lying in bed. Allow the color indigo to flow over the entire bedroom wall. If you have trouble visualizing the color, get a sheet of indigo construction paper and place it on your wall.

Finally, if you notice or feel any of these sensations, it means your Third Eye is imbalanced: busy bee mind, problems with self-reflection, work related issues family issues, or difficulty in maintaining an open mind. Don't panic. Kick back and go into mindful meditation. Solfeggio scale at 528 Hz works very well for meditation.

The act of speaking your intentions aloud shifts them from wishful thinking to action.

CHAPTER SIX
THE ROLE OF VIBRATION

There's a lot of chatter these days about vibration and its role in healing, in changing realities, and in creating through intentions. At the most simple level, vibration is the repetitive motion of an object. Modern science tells us that all things vibrate including the universe itself. Scientific studies discuss such things as Hz, oscillation, elastic body or medium. Hz is probably the most often used in the literature surrounding vibration. What then is Hz? According to the Wikipedia, "The **hertz** (symbol: Hz) is the derived unit of frequency in the International System of Units (SI) and is defined as one cycle per second. It is named for Heinrich Rudolf Hertz, the first person to provide conclusive proof of the existence of electromagnetic waves. Hertz is commonly expressed in multiples: kilohertz (10^3 Hz, kHz), megahertz (10^6 Hz, MHz), gigahertz (10^9 Hz, GHz), and terahertz (10^{12} Hz, THz)."

Consider this for a moment: The typical air at normal room conditions, has its average molecules moving close to 1000 MPH. Also, remember, the speed of sound is determined by how fast the molecules move between collisions [that creates the sound]. With everything vibrating, you can readily see why your intention becomes all important.

Tim Welsh, Professor of Kinesiology and Physical

Education, University of Toronto [22] suggests that neurons that link the spinal cord to the muscles can travel up to 270 miles per hour. Imagine how fast the thought is that sent the message for the muscle to move. We are also told that a transitional kinetic energy molecule mass travels at 667 MPH. The speed of sound is a bit faster. The importance of these figures is they reinforce the premise that vibration has a huge impact on intention. It is the vehicle by which intention is sent into the universal energy to create a physical and emotional rendition of your desire.

Since we have a notion of the speed of things vibrating how long does it take to manifest something? Daylle Deanna Schwartz gives the following answer: "There is no definite answer because ***it depends on you*** [The bold italics is mine.] It's different for everyone and for every desire. A bigger goal may take longer to reach, but it may not for some people. The short answer to how long does it take to manifest desires: It will take as long or as short as it takes you to release your resistance to having it and then getting your vibration high". In the chapter titled Activities you will find some exercises to help you raise your vibrations.

Leona Henryson in "Vibrate the Cosmos—Your Thoughts & Intentions Can Create Your Path" states, "You are connected with all of the abundances that are in the Universe - perfect health, perfect wealth, perfect everything! Your vibrations are the same vibrations running through everything. Vibrate that Cosmos with your positive energy and thought; claim what is yours today, right now. Keep claiming it, seeing it, and act as if you already have it." [23]

We are reminded that one of the foremost minds of all times, Albert Einstein tells us that "Everything in life is vibration." Don't you think we should listen? Maybe, just maybe we should heed his wisdom. Einstein said it, but IT is the law of Nature—everything vibrates. There is nothing that does not vibrate. Even the words on this printed page.

The higher and more direct your own energy vibration frequency resonates, the more you will attract the same vibration from the Universe.

CHAPTER SEVEN
GRATITUDE

Gratitude, like so many words, has had its meaning corrupted by over use. Simply put, gratitude is the quality of being thankful, that is, one shows a decided willingness to express an appreciation for a kindness. I will add an appreciation for life. Ralph Waldo Emerson put it this way: "Cultivate the habit of being grateful for every good thing that comes to you, and to give thanks continuously. And because all things have contributed to your advancement, you should include all things in your gratitude."

Robert Emmons proposes two components to gratitude. First, the one that is generally at the top of most lists, is "an affirmation of goodness." He claims the second component of gratitude is the recognition of the source of goodness is outside of ourselves. Obviously, one does not have an affirmation of negativity (badness). The recognition of a source of goodness outside of ourselves is simply an acknowledgment of the wondrous effects of the energies of the Universe. There is never anything wrong with saying *thank you* as long as it is sincere.

Despite our good "intentions" there seem to be issued in getting our gratitude to bloom. According to Professor Emmons "the act of gratitude is also viral and has been found to greatly and positively influence not just relationships, but one's own emotional status. Research has proven that gratitude is essential for happiness, but modern times have regressed gratitude into a mere feeling instead of retaining its historic value, a virtue that leads to action." [24]

And therein lies the big issue with gratitude and intention. Because of what I choose to call a malaise that has and is continuing to spread across the United States genuine gratitude has become as rare as the birth of a white buffalo. Just what is this malaise? It is the belief that we are owed—a living, a job, a place to live, health care. In the present, *thank you* has become a robotic answer lacking in sincerity and belief. We have evolved into an "I" society. The negative energy generated by such beliefs and behavior leaves little room for intention to blossom into reality.

If you truly want your intentions to come to fruition

be grateful. Don't let a sense of false guilt stand in your way. Don't let resentment cloud the goodness

you have received.

CHAPTER EIGHT
INTENTION? AFFIRMATION?

An intention, if you will remember is a state of mind in which there is a commitment, a fulfilling of a particular action, or desire. An affirmation is an assertion that something is true; a positive statement that describes the desired situation. Generally, an affirmation is repeated many times as a way of impressing it in the one's subconscious mind. It functions as a trigger point for positive action. This is significant since experts predict there are 60 to 80 thousand thoughts per day for the average person. That's a whopping 2500-3300 per hour. Imagine, if you will, the power held here if you concentrated on just one thought. It is mind boggling, to say the least.

An affirmation is a statement that your intention is true. What specifically does an affirmation do? According to Remez Sasson in "What are Affirmations and How to Use Them" affirmations motivate, keep your mind focused on your intention, and influence the subconscious mind and activate its powers. For an affirmation to be true, it should always be stated in the present tense. Instead of saying "I want to be confident" say "I am confident" or instead of saying "I will be grateful" say "I am grateful." However, in "How Positive Affirmations Work," on the *Trinity Affirmations Blog* [25] it is suggested that there are potential ways of stating one's affirmation: Present tense affirmation, future tense affirmation, and natural affirmation. The first two are self-explanatory; the third, natural affirmation requires a brief explanation. According to the article, natural affirmations are timeless that is they are a part of your core belief system.

Jo-Ann Downey in "Intentions versus Affirmations4" of the "Intention Series" states: "I experience intentions as being both in the present and the future. Like walking down a path while seeing myself on the same path in front of me. Affirmations are definitely in the present tense."

Because I firmly believe that you can manifest more than money and other material goods, I am providing a few examples of affirmation that are health based.

I am healthy.
I am energetic.
I am at peace with myself.

The bottom line is you must have an affirmation of your intention. If you do not, the intention hangs up and is unfulfilled. I certainly agree one should use an intention/affirmation every day, a mantra if you will. Doing so will eventually bring significant changes to your life. It's similar to daily doing an exercise routine

> **Successful people do what unsuccessful people are not willing to do. Don't wish it were easier; wish you were better.**
> Jim Rohn

CHAPTER NINE
FAILURE

After I had completed one of my talks on manifesting, a member of the group asked: "I have tried and tried and nothing happens. I have followed the procedures to the letter. Why doesn't it work? " I hear that question quite often: *Why doesn't it work?*

No matter who you are, no one likes failure. All too often we don't really look at the cause or causes of that failure. Unfortunately, we are all too ready to blame others. Some blame the Universe while others blame God or some other derivative of a supreme deity.

There are four general reasons for failure to manifesting one's intention. First, we tend to focus only on the end result—the goal. Zack Michael reminds us "to not only focus on the goal but to focus on everything in between." [26] Second, we get completely caught up in fantasizing our world if we get our intention. Third, we forget there are plateaus in our progress. We become impatient and turn to negative thinking. Fourth, is not showing gratitude. Even though Zack Michael tells us to focus on more than just our goal, he also tells us to do this with gratitude. (See Chapter 8 for gratitude.)

Chris Cade in his eBook, *The Law of Attraction Hoax*, states "too much emphasis is placed on affirming positivity and raising vibration positivity but not enough energy is invested in the present and in the moment." A reality check is always a good practice and when that is not done, intention failure is set in motion.

Ray Williams in a *Wired for Success* article titled "Why Goal Setting Doesn't Work makes the following observation: "Despite the popularity of goal setting, there is compelling evidence that regardless of good intentions and effort, people and organizations consistently fall short of achieving their goals. More often than not, the fault is attributed to the goal setter. But the real problem may be in the efficacy of goal setting itself." [27] Williams has aptly laid out a crucial reason for intention failure—our capacity to produce the desired effect. Setting a goal is fine as long as it is the end result of that goal that one intendeds.

According to Douglas Vermeeren at ReliablePlant.com in "Why people fail to achieve their goals" state "Approximately 80% of people never set goals for themselves. Of the 20% of the population that does set goas, roughly 70% fail to achieve the goals they have set for themselves." He attributes the failure to a lack of understanding of the goal-setting process. [I interpret goal as intention.] All too often, the intention is not realistic. For example, if you set your intention to be the world's wealthiest human being and you have no experience in business, technology, or inventiveness, you have slated failure.

Another major causes of intention failure is a lack of commitment. Approaching manifesting in a haphazard way and not repeating your intention mantra on a specific and regular basis boldly announces to the Universe that you are not really committed to achieving your intention. Remember, the Universe is energy and it responds to positive energy. If you are not supplying your personal positive energy to your intention, the Universe will respond in like manner and your intention will be a failure. Be consistent.

An article published in Mind Tools.com titled "Eight Common Goal Setting Mistakes" provides an excellent overview of why intention fails. These, written by the Mind Tools Content Team, are worth repeating here.

1. Setting Unrealistic Goals
2. Focusing on Too Few Areas
3. Underestimating Completion Time
4. Not Appreciating Failure
5 Setting "Other People's Goals"
6 Not Reviewing Progress
7. Setting "Negative" Goals
8. Setting Too Many Goals.

The fourth mistake, "Not Appreciating Failure" appears to be an odd reason for intention failure. A closer examination suggests a simple fact of life: we all fail at something at some time during our lifetimes. During those times, accept them as a teaching-learning situation. Don't dwell on the failure. Move on but be sure you understand how you failed so you don't repeat it again. Experience has shown that the eighth mistake is a common cause of intention failure. People tend to create a shopping list when it comes to goal setting. I want to exercise more, I want to eat better, I want to lose weight, I want, I want, I want. You get the picture. A better intention would be I want to increase my exercise time ten minutes per session.

A major mistake that people make and one that nearly guarantees failure is they visualize happiness as future based. As I have said in my books, articles, and lectures, happiness is not a goal. You don't say "I am going to be happy next year." Happiness is a now thing. You don't work toward it! And finally, bringing your intention into reality is more than just wishful thinking. You just don't make a wish.

Patience is a virtue and it certainly is when it comes to successful intention. Being overly anxious, or too busy to do the dance results in failure. People want to know how long it takes an intention to work. You won't like the answer. It takes as long as it takes. You cannot hurry the Universe. The Universe in its infinite wisdom will test you and will provide clues that it is processing your intention. Unfortunately, people tend to overlook the clues. An illustration may be helpful. Suppose you have intended money, say ten thousand dollars. A few days go by and nothing. ?As you are walking to your car from a local store, you see a quarter laying on the ground next to your car. It wasn't there when you exited your car. Take that as a sign that your intention is in process.

Lar Collen in "Manifesting your desires using Reiki" states, "We must not doubt the process. Doubt happens to be one of the worst enemies of progress in any field of specialty." [28] This hold especially true manifesting your intention. If you are doubtful, you might as well hang it up.

Holographic Consciousness [29]

The illustration, Holographic Consciousness, provides an excellent example of human energy impacting Universal Energy. When you make an intention and do so for the purpose of manifesting the desired outcome, you are sending your energy out to the Universe; there to connect and to ultimately direct that energy to create what it is you desire. Use this image as a focal point to help you materialize your intention.

CHAPTER TEN
USING CRYSTALS IN INTENTION

The earth, world, and the universe are all vibration energy based. Crystals come from the earth and they are infused with that same magical energy. Crystal authorities generally agree that a major value lies in their ability to increase or amplify energy surrounding them. That includes the energy required to create and send intentions out into the Universe.

In addition to amplification of surrounding energy, crystals help to align our physical vibrations as well as our psychic vibrations with our intention(s). Thus, they become important allies in bringing forth what it is we desire.

Because there are hundreds of different crystals with many uses and or purposes it would require another book to include them. My intent here is to include the most powerful, what they do in terms of manifesting your intention(s), and how to use them

Amazonite helps to manifest clear communication, amplifies heart wisdom. enhances creativity. This crystal is generally small enough to allow you to carry it in a change purse, shirt pocket. Don't place it in a drawer and forget about it.

Amethyst is a popular crystal. Its energy helps promote the expansion of consciousness thus making your intention stronger. It may be likened to a GPS; it points you in the direction of your intention. Place two or three Amethyst crystals around you as you mediate. If you are seated in a chair, place an Amethyst crystal under each bare foot.

Carnelian, a power crystal is excellent for bringing creative balance and self-confidence. One of its other attributes, which may be helpful in bringing about an intention, is its function to enhance one's ability to love your Self. If you are a bit timid about manifesting your desires I suggest you place Carnelian under your pillow at night. Its orange/red color is indicative of its fire.

Heulandite Stilbite is a great crystal to help you

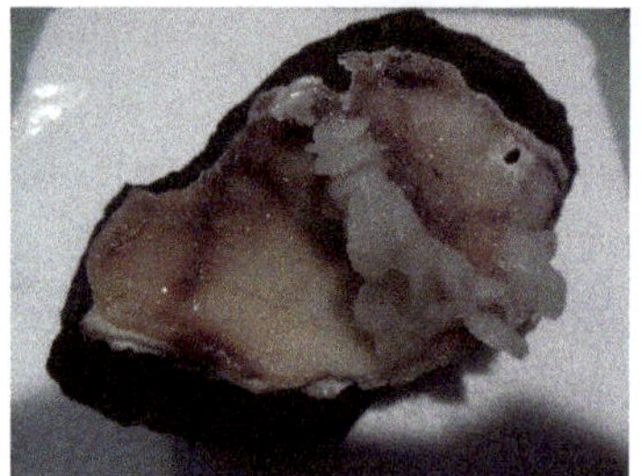

increase your vibrations. It also provides strong energy for the 3rd Eye. Good for meditation. Place it on a nightstand, near your computer, or your chair as you watch television.

Howlite is a powerful crystal and promotes calm

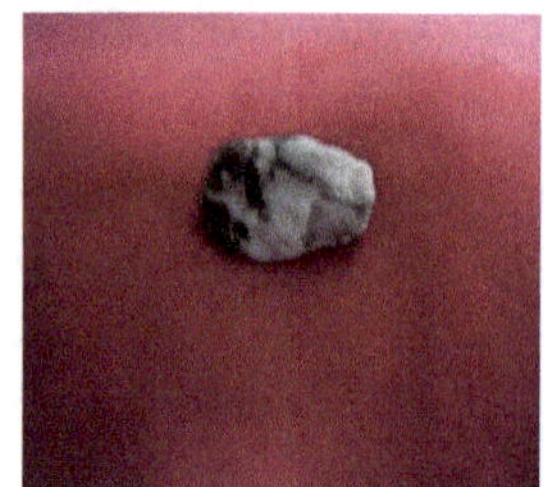

communication and helps you express your emotions. Keep this near your work station, in a desk drawer at work, or tuck it under your pillow at night.

Labradorite is an excellent crystal to have on

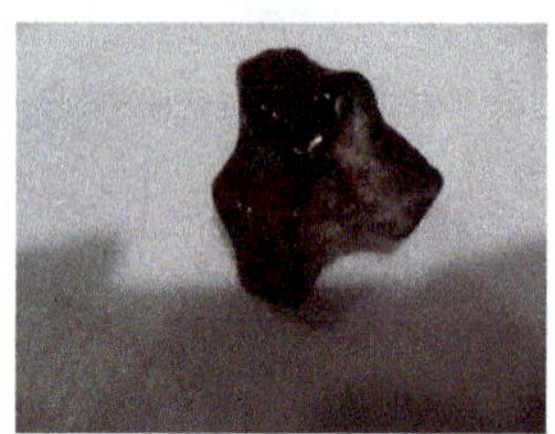

hand when you express gratitude. It enhances your 3rd Eye and heightens your intuition. Keep it near you when you express your gratitude. If you are so inclined, hold it in your dominate hand.

Quartz, both clear and Rose, are high energy generating crystals. They are powerful in helping you manifest your intention(s) no matter the type. To use either one of these, I suggest you go into a meditative state.

Place your right hand on your knee, palm up. Place the crystal in that hand. Do not squeeze the crystal. Meditate for at least 10 minutes; 15 minutes would be better. Rather than checking your watch to see if the time has elapsed, set an alarm on your cellphone, or alarm clock.

During your meditation, say your mantra which expresses your intention. You may say this out loud or to yourself. Some people record their mantra and using earbuds play it as they go about their daily routine.

A cautionary tale about meditation. Do not concern yourself if you can't clear your mind.

Very few people can. I am an advocate of Mindful Meditation. Saying your mantra will help you avoid going on a lengthy mental journey. Let the thoughts come in; acknowledge them and move on.

In addition to these seven crystals, the following crystals that may be useful to you.

Pyrite helps eliminate what is called poverty consciousness.

Green Jade helps you to focus.

Malachite good for courage. In this case the courage to realize your intention.

Citrine is an excellent confidence booster.

Tiger's-eye is probably the one stone every person who manifests should have with them. It is a powerful protector of your energy; helping to keep it from being absorbed by other external factors.

Be sure what you intend is positive because what you intend comes back to you.

CHAPTER ELEVEN
ESSENTIAL OILS AND INTENTION

What is an essential oil? The National Association for Holistic Aromatherapy provides the following rather long definition. "The term *essential oil* is a contraction of the original *quintessential oil*. This stems from the Aristotelian idea that matter is composed of four elements, namely, fire, air, earth, and water. The fifth element, or quintessence, was then considered to be the spirit or life force." [30] Thus, we have the life force, the oil, of plants.

The International Organization for Standardization defines an essential oil as a product formed by the distillation of plant substance with either water or steam or by mechanical processing. The oil from the plant is separated from the water.

In simpler terms, an essential oil is the concentrated version of the natural oils in plants.

During one of my essential oil classes taught by Aromatherapist, Susanna Mantis, I asked her why aroma? Why isn't what we are being taught called "essential oil therapy?" As it turned out, a French chemist, Dr. Rene-Maurice Gattefose is considered the father of modern day aromatherapy and is credited with creating the term aromatherapy in 1928.

However, the use of plant oils for healing has been traced back at least 3,000 years. Some historians suggest their use goes back at least 6,000 years. Whatever the date, we know essential oils have been used in healing practices for a very long time.

Adding essential oils to your intention helps, in a positive way, to bring your intention into manifestation. Essential oils are powerful contributors to your potential success in manifesting your intention. First, essential oils help your body to raise its bio-frequency, that is, its vibration. Second, essential oils help you get in sync with Universal energy.

Science has revealed that all living things have an electrical frequency. It has also revealed that all things, animate and inanimate vibrate—the Universe vibrates. Essential oils are an important aid to successful intention. Low range essential oils provide physical benefits, middle range vibrations effect the emotional realm, and high frequency essential oils have spiritual benefits.

The late Bruce Tainio of Tainio Technology determined that essential oils measured from 52 MHz to 320 MHz. Remember a Hertz is a unit of frequency equal to one cycle per second. This becomes important to you as you determine which essential oils you need to increase your vibration as you intone your intention. Tainio offers the following Hertz information about these oils.

Rose	320MHz
Lavender	118 MHz
Myrrh	105 MHz
Sandalwood	176MHz
Helichrysum	320 MHz
Frankincense	147 MHz
Chamomile	105 MHz [31]

The following essential oils help to stimulate the conscious mind and halt negativity: Basil, geranium, juniper, neroli, pine, labdanum, cedarwood, bergamot, and clary sage.

As an advocate for the use of essential oils in improving the success ratio of intention as well as for over-all healing, I am including what constitutes therapeutic oil and what is 100% pure essential oil. One of the issues facing today's essential oil consumer is the lack of an official grading system that denotes an oil as therapeutic as opposed to one that isn't. Anyone who produces essential oils and sells them can call them therapeutic. And this is generally done for the sole purpose of marketing. Beware of those essential oils offered for sale in the local grocery store.

One hundred percent essential oil may simply mean it contains only one oil and no emulsifiers such as olive oil, jojoba oil, or cannabis oil. Generally, the "pure" oils are very strong and may cause some discomfort. The question you should ask is what percentage is the oil. I know of no aromatherapist who recommends taking the 100% pure oils internally.

They are fine to use in a diffuser. Note that herbal elixirs are not the same as essential oils. The elixirs are taken with water or fruit juice and are for internal use. Always check with your medical professional before ingesting any essential oil. And while you are at it, also check about any use of a crystal elixir.

CHAPTER TWELVE
HERBS AND INTENTION

An herb is any plant with leaves, seeds, or flowers used for flavoring, food, medicine, or perfume. The herbs that will be the focus of this chapter fall into the area of flavorings, food, and medicine. I do note that some writers about herbs include several poisonous plants. I find that tends to create potential confusion so they will not be included here. As with crystals and essential oils, check with your medical professional before using herbs. There are potential issues due to allergies.

Combine the natural energy of the earth in which the plants are grown with that of the sun and add your specific intention you have a very powerful energy force to send out into the Universe.

Several herbs that most households will have within their kitchens are excellent in making intentions for wealth and health.

Allspice is good for changing your luck, to bring money and to induce healing. Besides using Allspice in your daily cooking I suggest you add a tablespoon full into a small saucer and place that on your night stand or computer. Actually, it would be a good idea to place it in both areas.

Cinnamon is also good for any intention set for increasing one's financial status. Put it in your food or hot beverages. If you have a place where you toss your spare change, add a tablespoon of cinnamon to a small clear plastic bag and place that where you toss your change. If you are going to do a meditation to enhance your intention, place a teaspoon of cinnamon in a cup of hot water. Place it nearby as you mediate.

Ginger is good for intending wealth, love, and increasing one's sensuality. Add it to your cooking and baking. It is available in the following forms, fresh, crystalized, powdered, or candied. Place a piece of crystalized ginger in your purse, coat pocket, in a desk drawer, or make a sachet and place it under your pillow.

Rosemary, long one of my favorites, is a wonderful addition to soups, pot roasts. It is found as an essential oil as well as an incense. If you are creating an intention to heal yourself or someone else, Rosemary is an excellent addition to use. Add a few drops to a diffuser in the room in which you are making your intention or add a few drops to a pan of warm water and soak your feet during the setting of your intention. To add to your cooking, add a fresh twig to the insides of a chicken, place in a soup, or on top of a roast.

Thyme is another excellent addition to your cooking. It is available as an essential oil, its leaves can be burned as an incense, or used as a tea or soaked in water, mashed in to a poultice. If you use it as a poultice, place it over the eyes or across the forehead. Thyme is wonderful for various health issues such as hair loss, poor skin conditions, and as an anti-inflammatory. Its essential oil can be used in a diffuser, applied directly to the skin, as well as added to foods.

There are more herbs that can be used to enhance your intention. A few have been mentioned to increase your financial status and health status. Is there a role for herbs and intention in the area of spirituality? Yes, there is a decided role. Calendula, for example, is. is a powerful spiritual herb that will bring healing as well as activate your innate healing abilities. Use it as a tea. Hibiscus tea brings you and your loved ones closer together as it heals past wounds. It opens the door for a spiritual renewal. One more is Rose tea. It opens your heart, making you more sensitive to the spiritual aspects of your life.

If you use any of these teas or other spiritual enhancer teas set the tone. Turn down the lights, play some soft music, take a warm bath and slowly sip your tea of choice. Quietly say what I call the Three B's Mantra; *I am bountiful, I am blissful, I am beautiful.*

Use this image of a shooting star as a reminder that you are made of star stuff. Latch on as you go through the activities to help you with your intentions and to bring them to fruition.

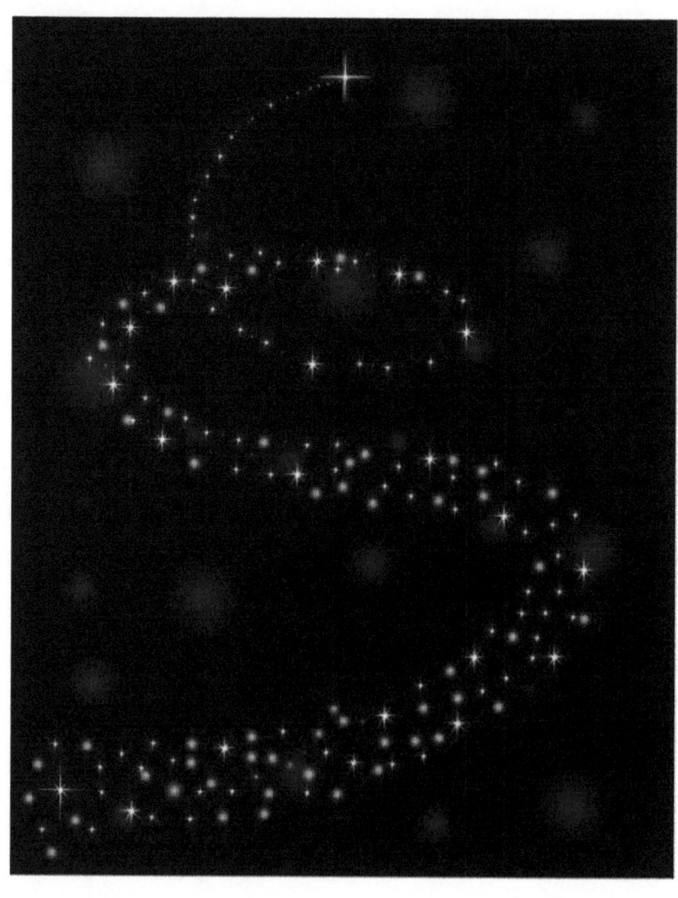

Magical Shooting Star by BSGStudio. All-Free Download.com

CHAPTER THIRTEEN
REIKI AND INTENTION

It is not my intent to recreate the history of Reiki or to become a party to the disagreement surrounding its history. Yet, I feel it is necessary to clarify a few salient points. Reiki is pronounced Ray-Key. Rei means universal energy and Ki means life force. All cultures have had and do have a recognized term for "life force." In Chinese it is *Chi,* in India it is *Prana, Mana* in Polnesia, *Rauch* in Hebrew,and in Jainism it is *jiva.* Both aspects of Reiki have a relationship to intention.

According to William Lee Rand in "What Is the History of Reiki?" published by the International Center for Reiki Training[30], there were "at least four other styles of Reiki healing being used in Japan prior to and during the introduction of the Reiki technique introduced in 1920 by Dr. Mikao Usui. Dr. Usui and his followers made that approach the standard. No matter which "style" of Reiki one uses it has one aspect that is all important and that is *intention.* Lar Collen in "Manifesting your desires using Reiki" [31] points out intention is the application of your will in directing your energy. The point being made is that you direct your energy with clearly stated intention.

At what point do you use Reiki? This is a matter of opinion but logic tells me that you begin drawing in Reiki energy before you make your intention. Remember, we are talking about a universal life force.

Your intention should be such that it will *bring no harm* to anyone, including yourself. But, you say, you don't know Reiki, how can I do a Reiki treatment on myself? The following steps will provide you the necessary information and as is with any new information, you need to practice and to be patient.

1. Settle yourself in a quiet place.
2. Relax. Stretch your arms and legs.
3. Take a three deep breaths, holding to a count of five between each breath.
4. Meditate. Use music. There are several excellent CDs available as well as Mp3 files.
5. Do this for about 15 minutes.

Once you have completed these five steps, you are now ready to add Reiki energy. I am giving you only two Reiki symbols to use.

The first is Cho Ku Rei (Cho-koo-Ray) Traditional use suggests you draw this symbol in the air and say the words Cho Ku Rei three times. You may draw this symbol on a piece of paper or on an index card. If you do, simply hold the card in your hand, or lay it on your lap if you are seated. Reiki practitioners generally say a "prayer" after the repetition. Basically, you are asking Universal Energy to come near. In this case you want

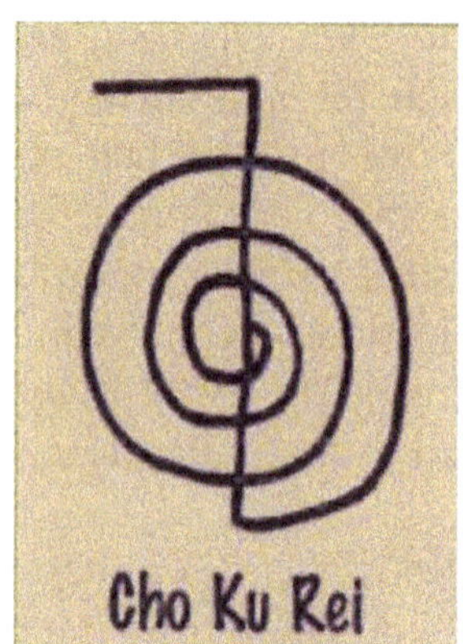

it to synchronize your energy with Universal Energy. Here is an example. You can modify it any way you wish.

Universal Energy come near and in your infinite wisdom do whatever is necessary to synchronize my energy with that of the Universe.

Before moving on to the next symbol I want to say a few things about how to say your prayer. Never beg! Always command! Notice the example I gave is a command. I am not saying "pretty please dear wonderful Universal Energy."

The second Reiki symbol that is useful in increasing your vibrational energy so that is meshes with that of the Universe is called Hon Sha Ze Sho Nen. (pronounced as Hon Ja Za Jo Nen) Generally, it is used by Reiki Masters as a symbol for distant healing and it is considered one of the most powerful by many Reiki practitioners. Even though it is generally used for distant healing, here it is used to connect to your higher self. It is there that your intention will become the most energized. It does take time. Patience is a prime prerequisite.

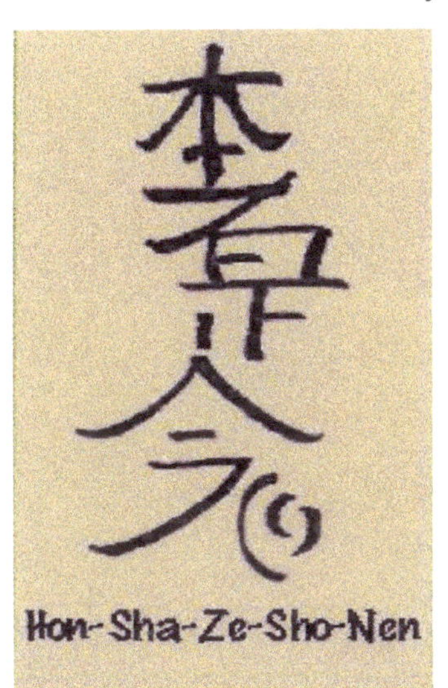

Again, draw the Hon-Sha-Ze-Sho-Nen symbol in the air or on a piece of paper. Here's a hint for your consideration if you copy the symbol on paper. Some Reiki practitioners suggest placing the palm of your dominate hand over the symbol as you chant its name. Say it three times. Then, say your chosen prayer.

After using one or both of these symbols and invoking your chosen prayer, be sure to close the open portal by saying thank you.

END NOTES

[1] Lipton, Bruce, Ph.D. The Biology of Belief. Santa Rosa CA. Mountain of Love Publishers. 2005.

[2] Reported by Brandon West, Contributor Walking Times. June, 25, 2014. Originally in The Power of Silence: Further Lessons of don Juan by Carlos Castaneda. New York. Washington Square Press. 1991. p. 12.

[3] Intention Series: How to Create Powerful Intentions in Very Smart Girls.com. 2007

[4] Mélange Publishing. 2015

[5] Beauregard, Mario and Denyse O'Leary. The Spiritual Brain A Neuroscientist's Case for the Existence of the Soul. New York. Harper-Collins Publishers. 2007. p. 33.

[6] Chopra, Deepak. "Five Steps to Setting Powerful Intention." The Chopra Center. SychroDestiny. 2015.

[7] Tabuka, Marla. *Setting Goals Isn't Enough: Setting Daily Intentions Will Change Your Life*. The INC Life. July 11, 2016

[8] Moffitt, Phillip. "The Heart's Intention" Balance for Individuals. The Institute Bookstore 2011

[9] Downey, Jo-Ann. "Intention Series: How To Create Powerful Intentions." Very Smart Girls.com. 2009.

[10] Dilts, Robert. "Positive Intention." *Anchor Points*. copyright 1996 by Robert Dilts.

[11] Walia, Arjun. Science Proves That Human

Consciousness and Our Material World are Intertwined: See For Yourself."

[12] Michio Kaku. The Future of the Mind. New York. Anchor Books 2014. P. 41.

[13] The Search for Life After Death, August 21, 2016.

[14] From Power of Positivity at https://www.powerofpositivity.com. Feb. 23,2015.

[15] Washington Square Press. New York. Reissue. 1991. p. 12. Quote also mentioned in Brandon West's article, "The Power of Intention. June 25, 2014. ©2011-2017 Waking Media, Inc.

[16] Human "Consciousness" Collapses the Quantum Wave Function in a Groundbreaking Study. Collective Evolution. June 7, 2017

[17] Staedter, Tracy. Here's Where Consciousness Exists Inside the Brain. Seeker.com. November 9, 2016.

[18] Fitnesshealtzone.com. Called: "Points to Consider During Third Eye Meditation. Here's the link: https://duckduckgo.com/?q=free+photo+of+third+eye+chakra+on+human+head&t=hw&ia=images&iax=1

[19] Based on "6th and 7th chakra-pineal ad pituitary gland-the opening of the Third Eye and NEW EARTH experience" by Myriel R, Aouine. January 24, 2013 in Chakras, Kundalini, Merkabah and Lightbody.

[20] In Gaia at www.gaia.com

[21] "What is the Third Eye? in Personal Tao at

https://personaltao.com. August 11, 2010.

[22] Christian Science Monitor, July 1, 2015

[23] Collective Evolution. December 26, 2015.

[24] Emmons, Robert, PhD. "What Gets in the Way of Gratitude?" in Big Questions Online. November 12, 2013.

[25] Trinity Affirmations at https://www.trinityaffirmations.com/blog/

[26] "Be Grateful for Every Step, My View" *Inside*. 8/28/2017.

[27] Posted April 11, 2011. Psychology Today.

[28] Published in Self Growth.com, The Online Self-Improvement Company. September 30, 2017.

[29] Appeared in an article by Brandon West titled Proof that the Human Body is a Projection of Consciousness. Waking Times, April 14, 2014.

[30] National Association for Holistic Aromatherapy. PO Box 27871 Raleigh, NC 27611-7871.

[31] German Chamomile

[32] The International Center for Reiki Training. 21421 Hilltop Street, Unit #28, Southfield, Michigan 48033. Email: center@reiki.org.

[33] op.cit. p. 48

Also by Norman W. Wilson, PhD

Textbooks:

Butterflies and All That Jazz with Drs. James G. Massey and Arthur J. Powell

Windows & Images: An Introduction to the Humanities with Drs. James G. Massey and Arthur J. Powell

The Humanities: Contemporary Images

Nonfiction:

Shamanism: What It's All About

DUH@ The American Educational Disaster

So You THINK You want to be a Buddhist?

Promethean Necessity & Its Implications for Humanity

The Sayings of Esaugetuh, the Master of Breath

Activating Your Spirit Guides

Shamanic Manifesting

The Shaman's Journey Through Poetry with Gavriel Navarro

How to Make Ethical and Moral Decisions: A Guide

Novels

The Shaman's Quest

The Shaman's Transformation

The Shaman's Revelations

The Shaman's War

The Shaman's Genesis

The Making of A Shaman

www.ingramcontent.com/pod-product-compliance
Ingram Content Group UK Ltd.
Pitfield, Milton Keynes, MK11 3LW, UK
UKHW021826270726
14058UKWH00001B/6

9 781786 951502